How Debt and Default Affect You

Philip Wolny

ROSEN
PUBLISHING®

New York

For my mother, Julita, an astute financial planner

Published in 2013 by The Rosen Publishing Group, Inc.
29 East 21st Street, New York, NY 10010

Copyright © 2013 by The Rosen Publishing Group, Inc.

First Edition

Library of Congress Cataloging-in-Publication Data

Wolny, Philip.
How debt and default affect you/Philip Wolny.—1st ed.
    p. cm.—(Your economic future)
Includes bibliographical references and index.
ISBN 978-1-4488-8343-1 (library binding)
1. Debt. 2. Debts, Public. 3. Default (Finance) 4. Finance, Personal.
I. Title.
HG3701.W66 2013
336.3'4—dc23

                                                    2012010254

Manufactured in the United States of America

CPSIA Compliance Information: Batch #W13YA: For further information, contact Rosen Publishing, New York, New York, at 1-800-237-9932.

Contents

Detroit's mayor, Dave Bing, holds a press conference regarding the troubling circumstances of the Detroit City Council's municipal budget at the Coleman Young Center in 2011. Detroit's debt problems have proved extremely difficult for its elected officials.

Introduction

Anytown, USA, has seen better days. Starting at any house in some of its worse-off neighborhoods, a visitor can easily tell the small city is suffering. On any street, at least a third of the houses are empty, while others have "For Sale" signs displayed. It is hard to get downtown because many bus lines no longer run or run only once or twice daily. Sanitation workers have gone on strike, the latest city employees to do so. Uncollected garbage litters the sidewalks. Police show up only for the worst emergencies.

Libraries, public health clinics, and community centers seem to close daily. In the fall, several public schools cannot afford to stay open. It becomes ever harder to find the money to cover even basic items for the annual budget. Many of those who can afford to do so decide to try their luck elsewhere. Those who cannot move away begin to see their city as a ghost town.

If this vision of a modern U.S. community seems unlikely, news stories from around the country prove otherwise. Detroit, Michigan, once one of America's greatest cities, faces many crises. One of the biggest is its tremendous debt. For many years, it has owed more money than taxes and other cash sources have brought in. This debt has resulted in shrinking services, school closures, and numerous other problems. The worst-case scenario is that the city could default on its debts and declare bankruptcy.

Detroit's problems are not unique. Cities and towns of all sizes across the country are facing debt and default, as are some U.S. states. Throughout 2011, international debt crises made the news, including the plight of Greece, whose national debt has threatened its membership in the European Union and ignited protest and other turmoil among Greek citizens forced to suffer severe cutbacks in government services and jobs. On a personal level, millions of Americans face crushing debt from credit cards, student loans, and mortgages. At the same time, the U.S. national debt, especially in the recent crisis known as the Great Recession of 2008, has presented lawmakers and citizens with many difficult choices about how to overcome it.

Debt and default—national, state, municipal, and individual—are serious problems. It is essential to define and describe them and how they affect the average person and his or her family. There are various forces at work that contribute to them, some of which can be complex and difficult to untangle and sometimes even frightening. However, armed with knowledge, you can better understand debt and default and begin to look at ways that individuals, communities, and nations are working to solve these crises and prevent them in the first place. This is the story of how debt and default affect you.

Chapter 1

Debt and Default: What Are They?

Debt and default have been in the news lately. From U.S. politicians arguing over the complicated problem of the "debt ceiling," to the European debt crisis, to the worrying tales of U.S. states, cities, and towns facing debt and default, the overall picture of what is happening might be difficult to understand.

Nonetheless, there are some basics to every type of debt and the threat of default. An everyday example might be a home mortgage. When buying an apartment or house, most people, rather than paying in cash up front, pay a small amount at the beginning and take out a mortgage or home loan from a bank or other lending institution to pay the rest. The amount owed is their debt. Usually the cost is spread over many years, with extra small percentage payments, called interest, added to each monthly payment. Automobile loans work in a similar way.

However, if people fall behind on their payments, they can lose their house or car. The debt they owe really means that the bank or lending institution technically owns their property until it is entirely paid off. If they cannot make the payments, they default on this financial obligation. When a bank takes back someone's house because of debt, it is known as foreclosure.

Personal Debt

Modern life includes many debt obligations. As with mortgage loans, consumers borrow money when they want to buy a car, for example. For many Americans, though, modern life in general has become ever more expensive. The cost of a college education has risen greatly in the past twenty years or so. Private universities are more expensive

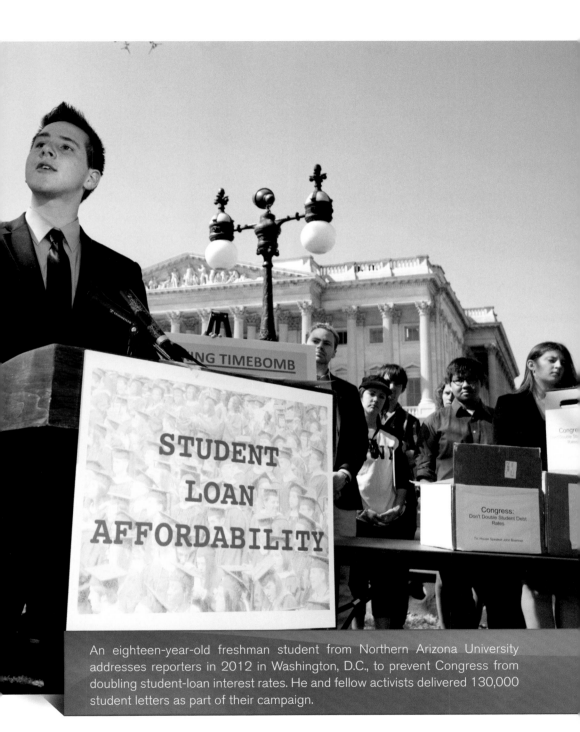

An eighteen-year-old freshman student from Northern Arizona University addresses reporters in 2012 in Washington, D.C., to prevent Congress from doubling student-loan interest rates. He and fellow activists delivered 130,000 student letters as part of their campaign.

than ever, while even local and state university costs have exploded. Federal and state grants for education shrank at the same time. Instead, millions of school-age students and their parents—as well as working adults—take out educational loans. Without these, many would be unable to afford school at all.

In addition, the costs of medical care, even for those who obtain health insurance through their jobs, have risen. For the tens of millions of Americans who do not have health insurance, treatment and hospital stays for major illness or an accident can run into the tens or hundreds of thousands of dollars.

The Credit Card Economy

Credit cards became a problem in the last few decades. Americans grew accustomed to spending more than they earned, a habit that caught up to them eventually. Still, some used them as an emergency measure in tough times. If someone is employed and doing fine financially, personal debt can be annoying but manageable. It is when things go wrong unexpectedly that many people fall into debt. A medical bill might prevent someone from making credit card payments on time. Late fees can start to pile up, and credit card companies penalize users with higher interest rates. Life can become a game of "robbing Peter to pay Paul," so to speak. If their situation does not change with a new job or other income, those in debt become caught in a race against time that they will eventually lose.

State, Municipal, and National Debt

A step above personal debt, municipal and state debts are also serious problems. Examined more closely later, they are debt obligations of communities that cannot keep ahead of their bills, much like individuals in debt. Although a person might suffer debt and end up in bankruptcy in a short time, it usually takes states and municipalities longer to reach insolvency. They may borrow millions and even billions of dollars over many years to pay for the many services that they need to provide to their citizens.

The shadow of Republican presidential candidate Mitt Romney is captured superimposed over a visual reproduction of the National Debt Clock during a town hall visit by Romney in Kalamazoo, Michigan, in 2012.

One step up from municipal and state debt is sovereign or national debt, the financial obligation owed by nations—specifically, the debt owed by their governments. Depending on the nation's size, its debt can run from millions into trillions of dollars. The United States has the largest debt of any country (more than $15 trillion), followed by the European Union and the United Kingdom.

Cause and Effect

Sovereign and municipal debt may also contribute to personal debt, with the reverse also being true. For instance, the collapse of the housing market resulted in many Americans losing their homes and declaring bankruptcy. But the crisis itself began earlier, partly because millions who had received mortgages began to default on these loans. A chain reaction occurred when the market crashed, making millions of homes lose value. At the same time, many mortgage holders saw their monthly payments rise tremendously; many more defaulted, and the process continued.

Even worse, many of the mortgages signed during the housing boom were subprime mortgages. These were sold to millions of customers without proper investigation of whether the borrowers could effectively pay them back. Banks cut these debts into financial instruments, or products, called mortgage-backed securities, which were then sold and resold. Many of the most important big banks gambled on these products, selling them like stocks and bonds. When people began to default on mortgages, these products lost much of their value. The subprime mortgage crisis

A bank customer takes out money from a Washington Mutual cash machine in Orem, Utah, in 2008. At the time, the bank was the largest casualty of the financial crash. It was seized by the government and broken up and sold to J.P. Morgan Chase.

thus threatened to bankrupt many of the biggest financial institutions in the United States. The controversial Troubled Asset Relief Program (TARP) of 2008, in which the U.S. government bailed out the big banks to save them from these increasingly worthless assets, contributed to U.S. debt.

Debt in a Wired World

The wired world people now live in, where information and money are transmitted and traded at lightning speed across national and international financial markets, has made all of its citizens vulnerable to debt. A financial or debt problem in another part of the world can quickly affect people many thousands of miles away. Easy credit for both individuals and governments can quickly turn into debt as financial high times crash into recessions and depressions.

This is why even those people and institutions that behave responsibly can suffer greatly from the wheeling and dealing of others. Imagine teens living in Vallejo, California, for example, who have parents employed by the city. Their parents might hold some typical debt like anyone else. But when that city faces bankruptcy, a similar chain reaction occurs.

Their parents lose their jobs, along with many of their fellow citizens, and perhaps lose their home to bankruptcy. Collectively, they all pay fewer taxes, leaving far less money for schools and other services. More city workers lose their jobs. Businesses depending on them to shop and buy things suffer, with some of these closing down. Private employers lay off workers. All the unemployed parents begin collecting unemployment insurance benefits.

Simultaneously, the state of California finds itself in a crisis, along with many of its cities, as was the case when the subprime mortgage crisis hit. The shockwaves from debt work their way in both directions.

What Default Means

Being unable to pay off debts is a problem that any person or institution can face. A government may face debt, but so can any private or public organization. These can include a wide variety of things: churches, school systems, small businesses like corner stores or laundromats, banks, multinational corporations, small towns, health clinics, and any other entity imaginable that spends and owes money.

The inability to pay off a major debt has different consequences for any of the above, although the general outlines are similar. A person or business that is unable or unwilling to pay debts goes into default. The people or institutions to whom the individual or business owes money are known as creditors. Often creditors will seek to get their money back from the borrower, known as the debtor. This step usually takes shape as some kind of legal action.

A customer walks by a Borders bookstore in San Francisco in July 2011. Borders filed for bankruptcy in February 2011, partly because of huge loan obligations and low profits, a recent problem for the print publishing industry.

Going Bankrupt

In the United States, a person or organization owing money can file for bankruptcy. For debtors facing bankruptcy, there are many protections, which can differ according to the situation. Whatever the scenario, it is an extremely uncomfortable process. This is true for governments and societies as well. If an economy or family's situation can be compared to running an automobile, bankruptcy might be considered a major engine overhaul after a major breakdown. Money fuels the economy, and debt and default can slow down or paralyze it.

Teens and their families are vulnerable to the effects of all types of debt. Personal and exterior debts bring both direct and indirect consequences. The effects may be as mild as having to save more and spend less. They can also be extreme, requiring a major change in lifestyle and habits. Emotional stress almost always follows financial stress.

Debt and default are tough experiences for societies as well. Russia and Argentina experienced debt defaults in the past two decades, and their crises even affected the international economy. America's current debt troubles do not seem as severe as the recently publicized problems that Greece is confronting, but they could grow worse. Such crises spread, affecting regular people. Just as personal debt causes stress within families, government debt leads to social stress.

Chapter 2

When Nations Face Debt and Default

Debt is a growing problem around the world, even for the world's biggest economies. National debt threatens the United States, while European nations have suffered in various ways during the recent Eurozone sovereign debt crisis.

Surpluses and Deficits

Government debt rises and falls in cycles. When more people work and earn money, the government collects more money in taxes. Taxes added to other revenues are called receipts. During times like the recent Great Recession, tax revenues fall. The federal government has less money for its expenditures, or outlays. If the government takes in more money than it spends, it is considered a budget surplus.

In the opposite case, the government takes in less money than its expenses, and thus it spends more than it earns. Just like a person buying a house, the government borrows to make up the difference. The amount of that difference (and the opposite of a surplus) is the budget deficit.

The Growing National Debt

In better years, when there is a surplus, politicians and citizens tend to forget about the growing debt problem. But

U.S. vice president Joe Biden *(far right)* meets with Chinese leaders, including high-ranking Communist party official Xi Jinping *(third from left)* at the Great Hall of the People in Beijing, China, on August 18, 2011, to discuss downgrading of U.S. debt and its resulting market shockwaves.

debt from previous years does not disappear—it keeps growing. According to the Center on Budget and Policy Priorities (CBPP), an independent group tracking the U.S. budget, the federal government took in about $2.2 trillion in taxes in 2010, but spent $3.5 trillion. The remaining $1.3 trillion was financed through borrowing.

The government borrows by issuing financial securities like bonds, savings bonds, and Treasury bills and notes. If

someone's parents bought U.S. savings bonds when they were young to help pay for college later, for example, that family owns a share of the total U.S. debt.

Individuals are not the only holders of debt. Others include national and multinational corporations, including lending institutions like banks, state or local governments, and foreign governments, including their central banks. Because China has become a major economic competitor, many Americans are nervous that it holds one of the largest single shares of U.S. debt. By the beginning of 2012, that amount was estimated at about $1.1 trillion, which made up about 9 percent of U.S. foreign debt. In total, U.S. debt was estimated at about $14.95 trillion as of September 2011, according to *Forbes* magazine.

Federal Government Spending

The U.S. government spends money on many things: the military; health care programs such as Medicare; retirement money in the form of worker pensions and citizens' Social Security retirement payments; the U.S. Postal Service; national parks; regulatory agencies like the Environmental Protection Agency (EPA); law enforcement agencies such as the Federal Bureau of Investigation (FBI) and the Bureau of Alcohol, Tobacco, Firearms and Explosives, many of which fall under the Department of Homeland Security; and many more. A debt default would dry up or freeze so much money Americans depend on. Losing the use of public services like mail or free recreation would be just the beginning. America would be in serious trouble if a lack of money prevented it from enforcing the law, defending the public from pollution and natural disasters, or even being able to provide medical care to the elderly or disadvantaged.

A National Debate

How to best handle debt has created much controversy. Many people believe that Americans cannot continue to spend as they have and must cut important government programs even if these cuts are extremely unpopular. Others believe the government must raise taxes, which many other Americans strongly oppose. Others believe in a third way, combining these two methods to fight debt.

Paying Off Interest

One problem with federal debt is the interest, which eats up billions of dollars per year. The interest owed on debt in 2011 was $454 billion, larger than most nations' actual revenues or spending. It is similar to someone owing a great deal of credit card debt. Each month that he or she is late in paying or pays only a small part of the balance makes it worse in the long run. The individual accumulates fees and finds it ever harder to get out from under the debt.

The Debt Ceiling

The summer of 2011 marked fierce arguments in Congress, which officially approves the federal budget, over the debt ceiling. This symbolic limit is the maximum amount of debt that the government should incur. President Barack Obama and congressional Democrats wanted to raise the limit to pay for the budget that Congress had already approved. Their opponents, including most congressional Republicans, opposed raising it without major budget cuts.

Although an agreement was eventually reached, many observers feared the "what if?" scenarios that might occur if the debt ceiling was not raised. The Treasury Department would continue to pay for government spending up to a point, but if it ran out of cash, it could have left the United States in a very bad position. The government could be forced to default on part of its debt, which could accompany a government shutdown.

Senate Majority Leader Nevada Democrat Harry Reid, flanked by colleagues, speaks at a press conference at the U.S. Capitol in Washington, D.C., on August 2, 2011, after a 74–26 vote to raise the U.S. debt ceiling and thus avoid national debt default.

Could the Government Shut Down?

A partial government shutdown due to budget disagreement happened in November and December 1995 and January 1996 during the presidency of Bill Clinton. As the *Washington Post* reported in February 2011, more than 260,000 government workers stayed home for more than twenty days, many of them left short of cash during the holiday season (though luckily they were paid back wages when the crisis passed).

Another government shutdown remains possible. Despite plans to keep important government functions working, including police and military personnel, other services could suffer. Veterans might not receive benefit checks, while new applicants would be unable to enter the Social Security system. Museums and national parks would shut down and passports would not be issued, among many other consequences.

What If the Federal Government Defaulted?

Washington, D.C.'s prominent Washington Monument is pictured closed to the public on January 4, 1996, a direct result of the government shutdown forced by Republicans to defeat Democratic President Bill Clinton on budget disagreements.

The exact effects of a federal default are unclear—mainly because it has never happened before. However, the Treasury Department warns that some early effects could be pay freezes for government workers and U.S. military servicemen and servicewomen, and freezes on countless other payments that U.S. citizens and businesses depend on.

Economic Meltdown

A government default could cause further economic catastrophe, including an economic shockwave even more powerful than the Great Recession the country suffered starting in 2008. With the many parts of the American economy interconnected in complex ways, several possibilities exist on how things could play out, with one or more happening simultaneously. International financial institutions and agencies would lower the United States' credit rating. This would translate into much higher interest rates for individuals seeking loans. Millions of people could be unable to afford new homes or cars or go to school, even if they had good credit and savings. Interest rates could skyrocket for credit card holders, too.

A Chain Reaction

Default could also cause a major stock market crash. Because so much retirement money, both for public and corporate employees, is tied up in stocks and other financial instruments, millions of retirement accounts could be affected. Even with economic safety

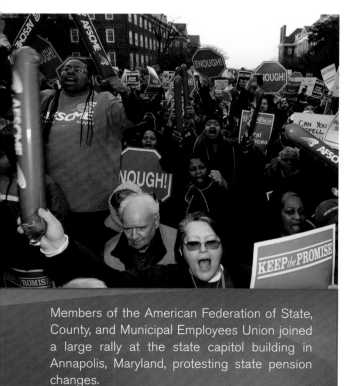

Members of the American Federation of State, County, and Municipal Employees Union joined a large rally at the state capitol building in Annapolis, Maryland, protesting state pension changes.

mechanisms in place nowadays that people didn't have during the worldwide Great Depression of the 1930s, the overall effect could be similar. Imagine dominoes standing on end in a long line: all it takes is one tap to send the whole line toppling down. With unemployment already very high, America could expect tough times indeed.

The European Debt Crisis

There are similar problems overseas. Although the United States and Europe differ in many ways, the roots of their current debt problems are similar. Both Americans and many Europeans experienced economic growth that ended up as a classic example of "too good to be true." The U.S. Great Recession, along with many different factors for certain European nations, helped contribute to some of Europe's largest economies suffering massive debt.

Decades ago, the problems of one country had less effect on others. In the 2000s, however, many European nations had adopted a single currency, or form of money: the euro. Currently, seventeen out of the twenty-seven member states of the European Union (EU) use the euro. This factor, along with other strong economic ties, also makes the entire Eurozone vulnerable to the problems of its individual members. One result has been tension among Europeans and among member states of the EU that have better economies and those with worse economies and higher unemployment. The unity of the Eurozone has been tested in 2011 and early 2012 by growing debt crises and perhaps most infamously, Greece.

The Greek Debt Crisis

Greece remains one of the world's wealthier countries, but its economy has been much slower than its fellow EU members, such as Germany. Like many nations (including the United States), it has balanced its budgets by heavy borrowing.

After the worldwide recession, tax revenues dropped and unemployment grew. Fewer people working meant that more people depended on money from the Greek government's "safety net." Simultaneously, Greece's creditors became nervous that its government could not handle its own economic problems. Many banks that lent to Greece raised interest rates. When credit-rating agencies downgraded Greek debt, the nation was threatened with bankruptcy. This emergency forced Greece to turn to the EU and the International Monetary Fund (IMF) to prevent it from defaulting.

Greece Boils Over

The EU and IMF bailouts contained very strict rules to force Greece to balance its budget. This meant huge cuts in pay for government employees, pensions, and other outlays that directly benefit the public. With the public already suffering, further cuts caused great national anger. Students,

seniors, and many other Greeks resented these tough rules, known as austerity (or hardship) measures.

As EU members and Greek government officials negoti- ated bailout packages throughout 2010 and 2012, Greek

Greek high school students protesting government austerity measures hold aloft a sign, loosely translated as, "With so much tear gas, where will we find the money for education?", a reference to police crackdowns on protesters, in February 2012.

The Celtic Tiger

Economic success (boom) and downturn (bust) are ups and downs that many nations experience. Ireland, a member of the Eurozone, had incredible growth between 1995 and 2008, earning it the media nickname "the Celtic Tiger." Much of the growth in the 2000s, as in the United States, was caused by the incredible boom in real estate. Many feared that when housing prices dropped, Ireland would truly feel economic pains. These predictions came true, especially after the Great Recession. By late 2011, the economy became smaller and unemployment rose a great deal. Ireland even began talks with the IMF and the EU to apply for money to help pay its debt.

protesters reacted. Riots flared up in the capital, Athens, and other parts of Greece. Several people have died, buildings have been burned down, and much antigovernment anger remains. Greeks blamed their own leaders for running huge deficits and mismanaging the economy. They felt they were being punished for their government's mistakes.

For the average Greek, the debt crisis and the tough solutions to it proposed by the government have meant great changes to income and quality of life. Older Greek citizens who depend on pensions have seen their monthly payments cut again and again. Thousands of Greek civil servants (government workers) have gotten pay cuts, have been laid off, or have seen their jobs threatened. Taxes have been raised on everything from property to goods, services, and food. Many Greeks complain they cannot afford the increases. Unemployment is at about 16 percent, and some Greeks with jobs have not been paid in months. Meanwhile, hospitals lack important supplies and schools are desperate for textbooks.

A Sign of Things to Come?

Greece's problems are a warning to the United States. Greece is a small nation, and similar problems surrounding U.S. debt would affect many more millions of people here. Americans fear that the political battles of their lawmakers have prevented real change and solutions to the many problems facing the country.

Imagine if tens of thousands, even millions, of federal government employees lost their jobs. Billions of dollars that help fund programs nationwide could be cut or eliminated altogether. For example, millions of Americans now depend on federal money for unemployment insurance extensions and to help pay for monthly food and housing expenses. Huge cutbacks could cause great political troubles that would dwarf the turmoil in Greece.

A U.S. debt default could lead to an economic depression that would cause even more pain than Americans have faced up until now. The examples of the Eurozone and the Great Recession will hopefully allow the United States to focus on making tough choices now, rather than waiting for problems to explode in the future.

Chapter 3

Debt and Default: States and Municipalities

You can see how debt and default affect the money that the federal government needs to provide services and how other nations, especially in Europe, face default. Drilling down deeper brings this problem closer to home. While the amounts of money dealt with are smaller, the problems remain the same. States, along with cities and towns—also called municipalities—can suffer from debt and the threat of default, too.

The Fifty States: Services in Peril

In the United States, most, if not all, important services and functions not handled by the federal government are often under state control. Like the United States itself, individual states depend on taxes and fees to pay for necessities; they also rely on federal money. From struggling small cities to

Protesters in front of Boston's Statehouse in 2012 demand the rollback of announced fare increases and service cuts. Huge construction costs on Boston's seemingly never-ending "Big Dig" highway tunnel were partly blamed for the debt facing the Massachusetts Bay Transportation Authority (MBTA).

the well-known debt crisis of California, debt and default threaten communities of all sizes.

The economic crises beginning in 2008 have meant that state budgets have grown smaller. With less tax money coming in, many states have been in financial crisis these past few years. Just like the federal government or private citizens, states must make up the shortfall between the money coming in and the money they need to spend; in other words, they must balance the budget. If a state cannot balance the budget, it must borrow money, putting it into debt. The longer a state continues to increase debt, the more dangerous its position becomes.

The Road to Debt and Default

States and municipalities can end up in debt by many varying routes. Much like individuals, each state or municipality behaves differently. Some may go into debt over many years or decades. Others make bad decisions whose effects are quickly seen.

Many states and municipalities overspent during better days, failing to plan for tougher economic times. In this way, they are like people. Moreover, just like people, they are not completely to blame. They are much like a married couple with children who took out a mortgage when they both had well-paid jobs. Suddenly, one or both of them end up laid off and must make do on much less money—and face sudden debt obligations, too.

Pensions: A Race Against Time

Municipalities have also mismanaged other finances. States and cities, for instance, maintain public pension programs, retirement plans that they promise to pay public workers, such as legislators, teachers, sanitation workers, police, firefighters and other emergency first responders, and numerous other personnel.

Many states and municipalities have used pension money for other expenses, hoping to put the money back in the future, but failed to do so. Others invested pension money too heavily in stocks, with pensions losing much of their value. Huge problems arose when it came time to pay off these pensions, and in many cases, retirees have had to bargain with their

An elderly husband and wife, having lost much of their retirement savings during the 2008 financial crisis, share a meal at an Ithaca, New York, soup kitchen. Millions of formerly self-reliant Americans have found themselves seeking help to get by.

pension funds to get part or all of their money. These financial pressures have bankrupted some communities.

What Do States Do?

State services and functions include many different things. Looking at these, it can be troubling to think that many services residents rely on could be severely cut or eliminated altogether. The nonprofit Center on Budget and Policy Priorities estimated in April 2011 that the fifty states, plus Washington, D.C., spent a combined amount of just over $1 trillion in 2009. Looking at the many goods and services that states pay for shows the frightening effects state debt and default will continue to have.

The Threat to Education

Debt and default have forced governments to cut funding in public schools from kindergarten through high school, as well as higher education (state universities and colleges). For younger students, these cuts mean fewer teachers, larger classes, and fewer resources such as books, computers, equipment, and more. Cutbacks also result in cancellation of extracurricular activities like school drama, sports programs, clubs, art, and foreign languages. Debt also causes school closures. The economically troubled city of Detroit has shut down dozens of its public schools since 2010. Plans to close up to half of its high schools means that Detroit teens may soon face overcrowded classes of sixty students each.

For state university students, school costs (tuition and housing) have increased for many years. State budget cuts are passed on

Students protest tuition hikes, budget cuts, and campus police brutality during a UCLA meeting of the University of California system Board of Regents.

to students. Tuition costs have increased greatly, and financial aid has fallen, too. It is students (and their parents, if they are helping out) with the least money that often cannot afford these increases. Many are unable to continue their education or cannot enroll in the first place.

Emergency and Essential Services

Other essential services are suffering nationwide. Without certain services, any community becomes a place few people really want to live in. Communities need police, firefighters, ambulance services for their safety, and sanitation services to keep streets free of garbage and snow. Sewers, roads, bridges, and electrical networks need maintenance. In better economic times, it was almost unimaginable to underfund these emergency and essential services.

A Growing Threat, State by State

For some of the state governments in the worst shape, the effects are felt not only by those who depend on services. If a state cannot keep ahead of its debts, many different people are affected.

One example is Illinois, which was reported in December 2010 to have one of the worst debt crises. Asked by television news program *60 Minutes* about Illinois' frightening fiscal condition, State Comptroller Dan Hynes admitted, "Pretty much anyone who has any interaction with state government, we owe money to." Examples include small

Legislators of the Illinois House of Representatives in the state capitol in Springfield fight a losing battle against huge debt in 2010, while trying to balance the state budget. Many either oppose major spending cuts or tax hikes, putting the budget process at a standstill.

businesses like pharmacies waiting to be paid for drugs they normally provide to citizens enrolled in Illinois' Medicaid program.

Illinois nonprofit organizations have suffered as well. Luther Social Services of Illinois was owed $9 million, which the state promised to provide it for helping elderly, disabled, and mentally ill state residents. Only after the charity spent all its extra cash was it finally paid; otherwise, it would have been forced to close. It was one of two thousand organizations owed about $1 billion by the state.

Living with Less

Because they are among the most vulnerable to begin with, citizens facing hard times may need state services more than ever. State money is one of the biggest sources of health care, food, and emergency services for the needy. Medicaid, the largest government program providing low-income people under the age of sixty-five with medical services, is funded jointly by the states and the U.S. government and managed by the states themselves. It is estimated

Harrisburg's Municipal Crisis

One recent municipal crisis has been the possible default of Harrisburg, Pennsylvania, the state capital. Harrisburg's main problem has been the money it owes for an overhaul of an expensive garbage incinerator. Because of missed interest payments, the city attempted to file bankruptcy in October 2011, a move denied by a U.S. bankruptcy court that November. It is possible that the state of Pennsylvania itself may have to take over Harrisburg's finances. Severe cuts to services, much higher taxes, and other extreme measures have become necessary.

that as many as forty-five million people nationwide would not have health care without it.

The Neediest: First to Feel the Impact

It is often the neediest people who suffer first, and often the most, when states cut important services. School lunch programs that feed disadvantaged students are often victims of budget cuts. Higher tuitions for state universities, combined with far less money available to help college students with financial aid, may be causing millions of low-income students all over the United States to give up on the dream of a college education.

California: The Golden State, in the Red

One of the biggest state debt crises has been developing for years: the fiscal crisis in California, the largest U.S. state by population and the largest state economy. In fact, if California were a separate nation, it would be among the top-ten world economies. But the Golden State has struggled against its debt problems every year for quite some time now. This includes about $612 billion in pension funds it owes retiring

California governor Jerry Brown delivers a budget proposal for 2012–13 at the state capitol in Sacramento, in January 2012, which included a 7 percent increase in spending he hoped could be achieved through a slight increase in income and sales taxes.

workers over the coming years, while it still expected a budget deficit of $9.6 billion for 2011.

California's efforts to "tighten the belt" have meant big changes for many people. Because state funding of the University of California system has been slashed, the approximately 230,000 students enrolled yearly have had their tuition tripled within the past decade. Salary cuts, layoffs, and other cost-cutting measures have affected thousands of employees in the system. The tuition increases have angered both teachers and students.

The public universities are not the only state-funded institutions where people are losing jobs. Many of California's 229 state parks have been closed or have had their staffs cut. This has affected not only park rangers and other state workers, but also the businesses that depend on hikers, campers, and other tourists.

For state workers who keep their jobs, many have been forced to accept pay cuts and mandatory days off (furloughs) every month to save money. Some estimate that public employees have taken at least a 15 percent pay cut.

The Snowball Effect

For governments of all sizes, falling behind on debt creates a snowball effect. Much like a person who misses credit card payments, a state or city that misses payments often must pay penalties, such as higher interest and fines. For governments that were having a hard time with their debt to begin with, the debt can grow much like a snowball gathering speed and size as it rolls down a hill.

Your Local Librarian

The ways that state debt and default can make life harder are both direct and indirect. It is easy to see how budget cuts can mean that your local library may be open only three days every week instead of five. But many budget cuts have consequences that affect the economy in diverse ways.

Say a library cannot afford to keep a librarian. He or she is fired and may not be able to find another job. Now, instead of a regular salary, that librarian may be collecting weekly unemployment benefits, given out by a state's department of labor. The librarian must cut back on expenses for luxuries, such as vacations, and sometimes even for necessities like food and shelter. If the librarian has children, they must also learn to live with less.

Governments and people that owe money find it ever harder to borrow more money in the future. The growing debt hole becomes more difficult to dig out of. Citizens suffer from the emergency cuts that follow. Cuts in education make it more likely that more citizens will be unable to get better jobs in the future. Default on debt can cause unemployment and economic depression, further shrinking citizens' earnings, and higher taxes on those earning less continue the snowball effect. If legislators and citizens cannot address these crises, states and municipalities could suffer for many years to come.

Chapter 4

What Debt and Default Mean for You

From the massive national debt to struggling small towns, debt seems to loom everywhere these days. For many reasons, personal debt and default (bankruptcy) are perhaps the most difficult to handle on an immediate level. Ultimately, debt crises and the hard times caused by sovereign and state and municipal default hit individuals the hardest.

A Bitter Pill to Swallow

The shock therapy and austerity measures surrounding the Greek crisis described earlier are not simply a foreign phenomenon. One sees that U.S. cities and towns face hard choices now. Even with the problems experienced since 2008, there is always the possibility that the nation, states, and cities could suffer separate but related debt crises simultaneously. With personal debt and default thrown in for

Camden, New Jersey, firefighters turn in their gear after they are laid off in 2011. The firefighters were among the 335 local government workers to lose their jobs in the city, including many emergency workers.

millions of people, the next emergency could easily prove a perfect storm of debt and default.

Even those who do not face personal debt themselves can suffer from its effects. In a town suffering emergency-service cutbacks, police and fire departments may be compromised. Imagine a loved one having a medical emergency and nervously waiting to see if an ambulance shows up. A long wait in a hospital emergency room could be the difference between life and death. The basic services people take for granted in modern life might unfortunately become luxuries for the few.

For young people, school cutbacks may only be the beginning of their troubles. After school, young people could lack community centers, pools, or other places to go. Parks may be closed, rundown, or unsafe for use. Money for youth job programs will dry up. Businesses cutting back or closing will hardly have the resources to hire adults, much less teens.

Personal Debt and Bankruptcy

Americans in debt come from all walks of life. Many have struggled because of misfortunes, such as unexpected illness, predatory lending, or a bad economy. Still others spent too much, living beyond their means.

Facing debt and the worst-case scenario of bankruptcy are among the most painful life experiences many people face. Losing one's car, home, small business, and life savings are events that can make life difficult for years, even for a lifetime. Debt ruins marriages, splits up families, and can cause health problems and even death.

The Hidden Costs of Convenience

Technology has allowed consumers to live beyond their means. Since credit cards became popular, personal debt has skyrocketed in the United States. Their convenience made it easier to spend money first and ask questions (or think about the consequences of purchasing) later. It is easy to become irresponsible using credit—many people pay only the monthly minimum on their balance. Even for small amounts, they may spend years paying it off and much more in interest than their initial purchases cost. Banks and other credit-issuing businesses have also gotten a terrible reputation recently for changing interest rates, including hidden fees and other questionable practices. Few people closely examine the many pages of fine print in their credit card contracts.

While many abuse easy credit, there are still many more well-intentioned people who fall into debt because of misfortune. In the last thirty years, and especially during the Great Recession, credit cards have become a last resort. Millions of people who have lost a job, experienced health prob-

President Barack Obama signs the Dodd-Frank Wall Street reform bill on July 21, 2010, at the Ronald Reagan Building in Washington, D.C., as Democratic legislators look on.

lems, or gone through some other traumatic event, such as a divorce or failed business, use credit to stay afloat. When they cannot find a new job or source of income, they dig their debt hole ever deeper every month.

Getting Used to Less

Teenagers face difficulties because of debt. Fifteen-year-old Jonathan Piña told the *Chicago Tribune* in April 2010 that his parents were forced to sell their home, moving their family into a two-bedroom Chicago apartment. For his family's sake, Jonathan avoided complaining about losing his privacy by sharing a bedroom with his two younger sisters. While dealing with his parents' stress, he also coped with his own frustration at not being able to find a job to help out. Luckily, he took part in a ten-week job skills program that paid a $400 stipend supported by After School Matters, a nonprofit organization. Jonathan's first check, he told the *Tribune*, taught him an important lesson about today's economy: "$200 is nothing."

Student Loan Debt

A college education has long been seen as a way up in the world. For many students nowadays, however, the cost of schooling means that they leave undergraduate and graduate studies with crushing debt. According to a February 2012 report in *Forbes* magazine, 2011 was the first year that student debt exceeded $1 trillion (surpassing Americans' credit card debt), with students graduating in 2010 owing an average of $25,250 apiece.

The Housing Crisis

Owning a home has long been a part of the American dream. During hard times, however, this dream has become a nightmare for many. Those facing hardships because of medical bills, unemployment, and other personal crises have used their homes as collateral for loans. The abuses of the subprime mortgage crisis have landed millions between a rock and a hard place, including long-time homeowners. For some, this has meant having to abandon the only home they and their families have ever known, moving into smaller quarters or depending on relatives to shelter them. Homeless shelters

A family, formerly homeless, is pictured waiting for a bus in Palm Beach, Florida, that will return them to Little Rock, Arkansas, to stay with relatives, using tickets courtesy of a local charity. Millions of Americans have gone through stressful changes during the Great Recession.

nationwide have experienced a rise in residents who up until recently considered themselves middle class.

The Worst of All Possible Worlds

One of the worst-case scenarios is facing various types of debt simultaneously, and many Americans face just that. Many of these debt crises reinforce one another.

Imagine an average working family, with both parents working, and two or three children. Perhaps both parents lost jobs in the Great Recession. The family already had thousands of dollars in credit card debt, plus a home mortgage and a car still not completely paid for. The mother falls ill and spends several weeks in the hospital, incurring a hospital bill of tens of thousands of dollars. Lacking health insurance, they take on a second mortgage.

Each month becomes a complicated, anxious game of bookkeeping. At first, they attempt to get by without charging more on credit. The family gives up every possible luxury, such as extra cell phones and even some necessities like new clothes. They must make the difficult choice between car payments and mortgage payments; they give up the car because a roof over their heads is more important.

The older sibling is graduating high school, and the family has a difficult sit-down: they cannot afford to help her with college. Instead, both siblings look for work. It is hard to schedule job interviews because the bus nearby runs only a few times each day—the city they live in has laid off several hundred bus drivers due to its own debts.

With unemployment benefits as the family's only income, the kids rely more on school lunches for food. Unable to pay the mother's medical bills, the family begins to receive threatening debt-collection phone calls. Soon, they max out their few remaining credit cards. It is uncertain how they will make it through the next few months.

Eventually, the wave of bills catches up to the family. They miss one mortgage payment, then another. Within a few months, they receive notice that their house is going to be auctioned. Once it is sold, they must vacate the property immediately. Perhaps the family moves in with relatives.

Bankruptcy and Credit History

Even those who make it through a debt crisis can experience negative consequences for years, perhaps even for the rest of their lives. Whether one defaults on credit card debt, loses his or her home, or eventually declares bankruptcy, these events can severely affect one's credit score.

Three companies—Equifax, Experian, and TransUnion—collect detailed information on anyone who uses credit, whether in the form of credit cards, loans, or other transactions, and assign a credit score for each individual. For better or for worse, they are used by banks, landlords, employers, credit card companies, real estate agents, and nearly anyone else one can imagine doing business with to judge the individual via his or her score. Going through debt problems can make it tougher to rent an apartment, buy a house or car, get a college loan, or otherwise function in society.

A client *(left)* reviews her credit report with the manager of a home-ownership center in New York State. Good financial counseling can both improve and even prevent a personal debt crisis.

The Emotional Toll of Debt and Default

Dealing with debt and default is not simply a financial problem. Stress, anxiety, and other negative psychological effects arise from owing money. This is true for both those who have become debt-ridden through little fault of their own, as well as people who overextended themselves irresponsibly. Debtors feel frustrated that they have made wrong decisions or that they have entered a situation where they have little or no control.

Even a family that was relatively happy before can suffer emotionally. Children might notice that their parents are arguing all the time or taking their anger out on the kids. Younger siblings might be confused or scared because of this unfamiliar situation. Students might have problems at school, including anger issues, getting along with fellow students, or the inability to fully concentrate on their schoolwork. For family members of all ages, financial stress also causes depression and anxiety.

Can Debt Make People Sick?

For adults especially, debt-induced stress can affect a person physically. Medical problems arise when people are anxious for extended periods of time, and sufferers might even have a hard time linking the two. A stressed-out debtor might experience headaches, backaches, and other pains. Other effects include higher blood pressure, as well as ulcers (small, painful holes in the lining of the stomach that arise from prolonged or intense stress). Otherwise healthy people can suffer from these ills. Those who have health problems already should watch out for these signs of stress.

Above all, it is important to remember that debt is a problem that can be overcome—in other words, that there is a light at the end of the tunnel. Family members, especially children, should try not to take things personally. If a relative is angrier, or even distant and isolated, they should realize that it is the situation that is affecting the person negatively and not one's own fault.

For those just beginning to experience debt problems who can still afford to do so, enlisting the help of a debt

A law student and volunteer counsels a homeless woman in a mobile legal clinic in Santa Ana, California. Free counseling services include help with common issues suffered by the neediest, including debt and bankruptcy.

counselor or financial adviser might be worth the extra money. Of course, many debtors do not have the resources for this. In many cases, free counseling may be available in the community to help families coping with debt stress. Community groups, churches, and both private and government-funded organizations might be a good place to seek help.

The Way Out

In the end, remembering that debt (and even default) are temporary circumstances is a good starting point to help cope with these problems. This is true not only for individuals and families, but also for communities, cities, towns, and even whole nations. Help is out there, and an important first step is facing the problem. Looking at some ways that people are trying to alleviate and overcome their debt crises and learning about tools for preventing such crises in the first place are also important measures to take.

Chapter 5

Rising Above and Beyond Debt and Default

Considering the trillions of dollars involved and the well-being of billions of people worldwide, debt and default can feel overwhelming. There are few simple solutions. The business-as-usual approach of recent years has not worked. Easy credit and thinking only of the present, and thereby ignoring future consequences, have resulted in governments and individuals drowning in debt. Solving these problems requires the efforts of international organizations, national and local governments, communities, businesses, and families and individuals.

Bailouts: Attackivng the Symptoms

In early 2012, the combined efforts of EU and Greek officials and international financial organizations resulted in a second bailout package to save Greece from defaulting on its debt. The earlier bailout of 110 billion euros (about $146 billion U.S.), plus another 130 billion euros ($175 billion U.S.) in February 2012, have saved Greece for now. It was feared, however, that another bailout would soon be necessary. Greece's depression is so great that few were confident of it recovering anytime soon. At most, they considered the latest maneuver simply a small bandage on a major wound, attacking the symptoms of an illness rather than the causes.

Forgiving Debt

As part of the bailouts, Eurozone leaders convinced many bankers to forgive around 50 percent of the country's debt. The logic behind this was that demanding that Greece's debt be paid in full could possibly destroy what was left of its economy. This would leave the country with even fewer resources to pay back anything at all.

Fighting U.S. Debt

The U.S. debt situation remains complex. The entire world would suffer in the event of future default of U.S. debt. However, time is running out to manage the problem effectively. Economists strongly believe that both government and personal debt combined have been big contributors to preventing the United States from growing its economy out of the Great Recession.

Resetting Priorities

Americans may need to deal with the world differently, mainly by rethinking their financial priorities. One proposal is to

Members of the transit workers' Transportation Union Local 100 join with Occupy Wall Street activists during a protest against unfair demands on workers by their bosses, economic inequality, corporate crime, and other issues, part of an ongoing movement by workers, students, and others.

reduce the size of the U.S. military presence around the world. Reuters reported in June 2011 that the combined price tag of the U.S. war efforts in Iraq, Afghanistan, and Pakistan could run to about $4.4 trillion.

Another idea attracting attention recently is raising taxes. Tax cuts implemented during the presidency of George W. Bush could be reversed, providing many billions of dollars to the U.S. Treasury over the coming decade. Taxes might also be raised on wealthier Americans and especially on multinational corporations. Higher taxes are always controversial, but the United States may have little choice if it hopes to reduce debt.

Many politicians have proposed that a balanced budget amendment be added to the U.S. Constitution. This could legally prevent lawmakers from borrowing to fund government expenses. In essence, the government could spend only what it had. One indirect consequence might be that it would leave extra taxation as the only real option to both run the government and begin to pay down trillions in debt.

Helping Homeowners

In February 2009, forty-nine out of the fifty U.S. states, through their attorneys general, came to an agreement with a few of the major banks on a $25 billion settlement dealing with various abuses claimed by mortgage holders in recent years. Critics have called for even greater financial penalties for the banking and mortgage industries and even jail time for some of the worst abusers.

Many Americans also favor a bailout of homeowners facing foreclosure and bankruptcy because they feel the mortgage industry abused its powers. They resent the fact that the federal government bailed out financial institutions and feel that homeowners everywhere still suffer with little concrete help. On the other hand, others claim that the blame also lies with those who accepted mortgage loans with little thought about the future consequences. They fear that more bailouts will just "reward" people for bad behavior when they should be held accountable for it.

Financial Planning at an Early Age

One idea is requiring that students of all ages—from the early grades through college—take classes on personal financial management, budgeting, and debt and default. This course of action will arm them with valuable knowledge of how to avoid debt and how to carefully review their obligations when they take out school loans, apply for credit cards, and even sign up for bank accounts. In the current financial crisis, many communities and organizations have begun such programs. One unexpected result of an otherwise terrible situation is that teens might learn from today's debt crises and hence prevent similar future disasters. If you have not heard of such programs in your own community, chances are you may soon enough.

Remaking Detroit

Detroit is one of America's worst cases of municipal debt. Its problems worsened after the housing collapse. Despite these hardships, some Detroit residents are hopeful, believing that there is nowhere to go but up. Residents could benefit from several ideas to shrink the city, which has lost a quarter of its population in the last ten years.

Plans are underway to tear down thousands of abandoned homes and bring residents closer together geographically. It is hoped that consolidating neighborhoods will help save money on transportation, emergency services, and infrastructure such as sewers and water and power systems. Detroit Economic Growth Corporation CEO George Jackson told *Time* magazine in March 2009, "We're going to have to really rethink land-use policies and do some pretty bold, innovative things." Taking advantage of the city's vacant land, Detroiters have embraced urban farming to feed a struggling population. Many residents believe part of Detroit's salvation will be growing small businesses, attracting artists and other creative people, and being a laboratory for new urban ideas.

Teens could both benefit and be part of these changes, helping their city become a model for the twenty-first century. Learning about healthy, sustainable food while working with community groups and nonprofits are great ways to save money, live healthy lives, and come together to overcome hard times. Detroit's incredibly affordable housing has also inspired efforts to involve underemployed young people in community rebuilding. Detroit's teens could help overcome their city's crisis with this do-it-yourself philosophy, inspiring hope and cutting the city's costs at the same time.

Getting Involved

Teens have a bigger voice in these issues than they realize. Though they cannot vote until age eighteen, they can get involved in various ways. One way is by writing to their local and national lawmakers. They can engage parents and other adults, such as teachers and community group leaders, and press

Taja Sevelle founded Urban Farming, a nonprofit organization that encourages the creation of gardens on unused lands to help revive communities. Here, Sevelle works on a farm plot in the northwest section of Detroit, Michigan, hoping to transform the decaying "Motor City" into a garden city.

An Ounce of Prevention

It is easy to blame one side or the other for the mortgage crisis and the housing bubble. However, stronger laws for both lenders and borrowers could prevent future crises. Mortgage applicants, credit card holders, and other consumers are often at the mercy of lending institutions that change the rules on loans and credit without warning or have contracts that are difficult to understand. Sellers of subprime mortgages have been widely accused of signing up homebuyers without determining whether they could take on the financial responsibility of a home loan. Credit card companies are known for aggressively marketing their products to college students and other young, inexperienced consumers. Legislators and public-interest activists have long criticized hidden fees, variable interest rates, and other tactics they believe are bleeding consumers dry.

On the other side, the culture Americans live in has favored instant gratification over personal responsibility for too long. Young people coming of age in the twenty-first century will need parents and responsible adults to teach them not to spend beyond their means. Every spending decision should be carefully considered.

them to voice opinions on how to fix the debt problems of both the federal and local governments. They can also express their ideas about how they believe national and local laws should treat those who are suffering debt and default.

Concerned teens are also chipping in. Rhode Island high school student Katherine Young held a bake sale in January 2010 to raise money to contribute to solving the national debt. According to CBC News, she wrote, "This is a serious problem and I am going to take a step towards solving it, one

High school students in Cleveland, Ohio, laugh along at a story being told by a retiree at a retirement center while giving the woman a manicure. The visit was part of the school's All-School Service Day, which gives students an opportunity to understand the importance of helping their community.

cookie at a time." The $50 she earned may not seem like much, but every little bit counts.

A similar spirit inspired Northbrook, Illinois, teen Katie Murphy to pitch in, too. In January 2012, ABC News reported that Murphy wrote to billionaire Warren Buffett. She offered a $300 contribution to pay off the national debt from her personal savings if Buffett agreed to match her gift. Buffett wrote Murphy back that he would do so.

Volunteers Needed

One great way for teens to positively impact communities in debt is by volunteering. If money has disappeared for much-needed services in their area, teens can still get valuable work experience, especially while helping those who are less fortunate. Aiding people who are elderly or handicapped, cleaning parks and streets, or donating their time to established charities, struggling government institutions, churches, or community groups are all possibilities. Teens who volunteer find it easier to find paid jobs later, apply for college, and generally derive a sense of pride and well-being.

Growing Up, in Debt

Older people often imagine that teens spend most of their time hanging out, shopping, or chatting online. In better times, this might be closer to the truth. Family debt forces teens

A teenager clears snow from a driveway. Some of the oldest and most tried-and-true ways for young people to earn money might be only a doorbell ring or phone call away. These are informal alternatives to seeking payroll-based jobs that might temporarily be scarce for young people.

to make sacrifices. Instead of new clothes, they settle for hand-me-downs or vintage clothing. They share bedrooms, especially if they need to relocate to a smaller home. Instead of going to movies or concerts, they borrow films from friends or the local library. Learning how to cook and investigating ways of saving money at the supermarket become valuable skills.

In tougher situations, teens may need to take on more adult responsibilities. Splitting a family up to go live with relatives is never easy, for example. Or one or both parents might need to relocate elsewhere for a time to find work, leaving older siblings to take care of younger ones. It is important that teens do not blame themselves or their parents for such misfortunes, but realize that it is hopefully a temporary situation in which they can help their struggling family.

Teen Entrepreneurs

Another adult responsibility for teens is earning money. With cash scarce and youth unemployment the highest it has been in generations, today's teens might find alternatives to traditional jobs. Starting a business, however small, is one option to help families or at the very least earn some pocket money without burdening parents. Services such as shoveling snow, mowing lawns, raking leaves, babysitting, walking or watching pets, washing windows, cleaning homes, and many other tasks can bring in much-needed income.

Teens can also use the Internet creatively to expand their moneymaking opportunities. Using their technology savvy, students can make money from editing videos, helping to design Web sites, tutoring younger kids, or trading items on sites like eBay or Craigslist.

Beyond just meeting their everyday needs, earning their own money teaches teens valuable lessons about financial management. It provides lessons that direct young people away from the seductive lure of easy credit and eventual debt. One of the United States' richest entrepreneurs, Andrew Mason, the billionaire founder of Groupon, started a neighborhood bagel delivery service as a teen and later sold inexpensive candy he bought wholesale to his fellow students. A quick Google search can give any intrepid young person dozens of ideas about how to start earning money.

Looking to the Future

The United States and the world seem to be at a crossroads when it comes to debt. Whether American society is destined for a future of struggle and suffering remains to be seen. Communities, governments, and individuals working together can potentially overcome the mistakes of the past. Teens will have to continue making sacrifices and reshaping their world; they are the ones who will inherit it. The work ahead may seem overwhelming, but remaining positive and finding creative solutions are key to avoiding a bleak world. In other words, you are far from powerless. Learning how debt and default affect you is one of the first steps on the road to making a better world.

GLOSSARY

austerity measures Strict rules imposed on a debtor nation to make it meet certain budget goals; sometimes also called "shock therapy" due to the financial pain the measures may cause.

creditor A person, organization, government, or other entity to which money is owed.

debt Money that a borrower owes to a lender.

debt ceiling A symbolic, maximum amount of debt that the United States should not exceed.

debtor A person, organization, government, or other entity that owes money.

default The state of being unable to pay a debt.

deficit The annual amount of monetary shortfall between a government's receipts and its outlays.

Eurozone The economy of many European nations, united by a single currency, the euro.

foreclosure The legal process in which a lender recovers mortgage money from a borrower as a result of the borrower's failure to keep up mortgage payments.

furlough Time off from work; in times of economic duress, it refers to days off workers must take so that the government can cut costs.

incur To become subject to as a result of one's actions or behavior.

insolvency The inability to pay debts.

interest A percentage charge on credit or a loan.

Medicaid A program run by U.S. states and jointly funded by the federal and state governments that provides medical and health-related services to low-income people.

mortgage A type of loan that assists those purchasing a home.

mortgage-backed security A controversial type of financial instrument created by combining numerous mortgage loans, many of them subprime.

outlays Money spent by the government.

predatory lending Dishonest actions carried out by a lender to entice or assist a borrower in taking a mortgage that carries high fees or a high interest rate, strips the borrower of equity, or puts the borrower in a lower credit rated loan to the benefit of the lender.

receipts Taxes and other revenues that fund government operations.

sovereign debt National debt owed by a sovereign, or independent, nation.

subprime mortgages Mortgage loans marketed to borrowers without proper investigation into whether the borrowers could successfully pay off the debt, widely blamed for the 2008 financial crisis. These mortgages are usually given to borrowers who have lower credit ratings than others and a greater risk of defaulting on the loan and who often are charged with higher interest rates.

surplus Extra money left over after a government has met its expenses.

ulcer A health condition in which a person suffers small holes in the lining of the stomach, often attributed to stress.

FOR MORE INFORMATION

International Monetary Fund (IMF)
700 Nineteenth Street NW
Washington, DC 20431
(202) 623-7000
Web site: http://www.imf.org
The International Monetary Fund is an organization made up
of 187 nations that fosters economic and monetary
cooperation and development worldwide. It has been
involved in implementing plans for debt repayment
internationally.

Make Poverty History (Canada)
39 McArthur Avenue
Ottawa ON K1L 8L7
Canada
(613) 740-1500
Web site: http://www.makepovertyhistory.ca
Make Poverty History is an international campaign compris-
ing many organizations united to ending poverty and
forgiving the debt of poor countries.

National Association of Mortgage Professionals (NAMB)
2701 West 15th Street, Suite 536
Plano, TX 75075
(972) 758-1151
Web site: http://www.namb.org
The National Association of Mortgage Professionals is a
trade group for the home loan industry.

Office of Consumer Affairs (Canada)
Industry Canada Web Service Centre
C.D. Howe Building
235 Queen Street
Ottawa, ON K1A 0H5
Canada
(800) 328-6189 or (613) 954-5031
Web site: http://www.ic.gc.ca/eic/site/oca-bc.nsf
    The Office of Consumer Affairs is the Canadian govern-
    ment agency that advocates for consumers, including
    informational resources on debt reduction.

U.S. Department of the Treasury
1500 Pennsylvania Avenue NW
Washington, DC 20220
(202) 622-2000
Web site: http://www.treasury.gov
The Department of the Treasury is the U.S. government
    agency with primary responsibility for managing govern-
    ment revenues through taxation and other policy
    decisions.

U.S. Federal Trade Commission (FTC)
600 Pennsylvania Avenue NW
Washington, DC 20580
(202) 326-2222

Web site: http://www.ftc.gov
The Federal Trade Commission is the U.S. government
    agency responsible for protecting consumers and fight-
    ing unfair business practices.

Web Sites

Due to the changing nature of Internet links, Rosen
Publishing has developed an online list of Web sites related
to the subject of this book. This site is updated regularly.
Please use this link to access the list:

http://www.rosenlinks.com/YEE/Debt

FOR FURTHER READING

Bellenir, Karen, ed. *Debt Information for Teens: Tips for a Successful Financial Life* (Teen Finance). 2nd ed. Detroit, MI: Omnigraphics, Inc., 2011.

Berlatsky, Noah. *The Global Financial Crisis* (Global Viewpoints). Farmington Hills, MI: Gale Cengage, 2010.

Casil, Amy Sterling. *Why Banks Fail* (Real World Economics). New York, NY: Rosen Publishing Group, 2010.

Connolly, Sean. *International Aid and Loans* (World Economy Explained). Mankato, MN: Amicus Publishing, 2011.

Connolly, Sean. *Money and Credit* (World Economy Explained). Mankato, MN: Amicus Publishing, 2011.

Dolezalek, Holly. *The Global Financial Crisis* (Essential Events). Minneapolis, MN: ABDO Publishing, 2011.

Donovan, Sandy. *Budgeting Smarts: How to Set Goals, Save Money, Spend Wisely, and More* (USA Today Teen Wise Guides: Time, Money, and Relationships). Springfield, MO: 21st Century Press, 2012.

Espejo, Roman. *Teens and Credit* (At Issue). Farmington Hills, MI: Greenhaven Press, 2009.

Fisanick, Christina. *Debt* (Opposing Viewpoints). Farmington Hills, MI: Greenhaven Press, 2009.

Foran, Racquel. *Developing Nations' Debt* (Essential Issues). Minneapolis, MN: Essential Library/ABDO Publishing, 2011.

Freedman, Jeri. *The U.S. Economic Crisis* (In the News). New York, NY: Rosen Publishing Group, 2010.

Furgang, Kathy, and Adam Furgang. *Understanding Budget Deficits and the National Debt* (Real World Economics). New York, NY: Rosen Publishing Group, 2012.

Hamilton, Jill, ed. *Bankruptcy* (Introducing Issues with Opposing Viewpoints) Farmington Hills, MI: Greenhaven Press, 2010.

Hiber, Amanda. *Alternative Lending* (Opposing Viewpoints). Farmington Hills, MI: Greenhaven Press, 2010.

Hunnicutt, Susan C. *The American Housing Crisis* (At Issue). Farmington Hills, MI: Greenhaven Press, 2009.

Kafka, Tina. *Poverty* (Hot Topics). Farmington Hills, MI: Lucent Books, 2010.

Kowalski, Kathiann M. *Poverty in America: Causes and Issues* (Issues in Focus). Berkeley Heights, NJ: Enslow Publishers, 2003.

Lankford, Ronnie D. *The Rising Cost of College* (At Issue). Farmington Hills, MI: Greenhaven Press, 2009.

Reef, Catherine. *Poverty in America* (American Experience). New York, NY: Facts On File, 2007.

Tardiff, Joseph. *Consumer Debt* (Current Controversies). Farmington Hills, MI: Greenhaven Press, 2010.

Thompson, Helen. *Understanding Credit* (Junior Library of Money). Broomall, PA: Mason Crest Publishers, 2009.

BIBLIOGRAPHY

ABC News. "Warren Buffett Agrees to Match Northbrook Teen's Donation." January 31, 2012. Retrieved February 2012 (http://abclocal.go.com/kabc/story?section=news/local&id=8526649).

Cancino, Alejandro. "Recession Hits Hardest for Kids Who Lose Homes." *Chicago Tribune*, April 26, 2010. Retrieved January 2012 (http://articles.chicagotribune.com/2010-04-26/business/ct-biz-0426-recession-kids--20100426_1_albany-park-children-homes).

Congressional Quarterly. "Raising the Debt Limit." July 5, 2011. Retrieved February 2012 (http://innovation.cq.com/media/debt_limit).

Congressional Quarterly. "Who Holds the Federal Debt." July 11, 2011. Retrieved February 2012 (http://innovation.cq.com/media/debt_components).

Costantini, Fabrizio. "'This Was Our Home'; Budget Crises Force Detroit, Other Cities to Close Schools." MSNBC.com, April 1, 2011. Retrieved February 2012 (http://www.msnbc.msn.com/id/37642350/ns/us_news-life/t/was-our-home).

De Rugy, Veronique. "The Municipal Debt Bubble." *Reason*, December 14, 2010. Retrieved December 2011 (http://reason.com/archives/2010/12/14/the-municipal-debt-bubble).

Glennie, Jonathan. "Debt Crisis: A Default in Europe Could Benefit Poor Countries." *Guardian*, August 9, 2011. Retrieved January 2012 (http://www.guardian.co.uk

/global-development/poverty-matters/2011/aug/09
/debt-crisis-europe-poor-countries-benefit).

Kelleher, James B. "In Detroit, Dreams of Civic Renewal
Collide with Hard Realities." Reuters, November 2, 2011.
Retrieved January 2012 (http://www.reuters.com
/article/2011/11/02/
us-detroit-comeback-idUSTRE7A17O920111102).

Lambert, Lisa. "Special Report: The Incinerator That May
Burn Muni Investors." Reuters, May 12, 2010. Retrieved
December 2011 (http://www.reuters.com/article
/2010/05/12/us-muni-investors-idUSTRE64B2
PM20100512).

Minnesota Public Radio. "What Caused the European Debt
Crisis?" December 9, 2011. Retrieved January 2012
(http://minnesota.publicradio.org/display/web/2011
/12/09/midday1).

O'Keefe, Ed. "What Might a Government Shutdown Look
Like?" *Washington Post*, February 17, 2011. Retrieved
February 2012 (http://voices.washingtonpost.com/
federal-eye/2011/02/what_might_a_government
_shutdo_1.html).

Reitz, Stephanie. "U.S. Teens Struggle to Find Elusive Part-
Time Jobs." Associated Press, January 10, 2012.
Retrieved January 2012 (http://www.mercurynews
.com/jobs/ci_19714613?source=rss).

Riley, Molly. "Vanishing City: The Story Behind Detroit's
Shocking Population Decline." Reuters, March 24, 2011.

Retrieved January 2012 (http://newsfeed.time.com
/2011/03/24/vanishing-city-the-story-behind
-detroit%E2%80%99s-shocking-population-decline).

Rooney, Ben. "Michigan Approves Plan to Close Half of
Detroit Schools." Money/CNN, February 22, 2011.
Retrieved December 2011 (http://money.cnn.com
/2011/02/22/news/economy/detroit_school_
restructuring/index.htm).

Sanburn, Josh. "What Would a U.S. Government Default
Feel Like for the Average American?" *Time*, July 11,
2011. Retrieved December 2011 (http://moneyland
.time.com/2011/07/11/how-a-u-s-government-default
-would-affect-consumers).

Sandbrook, Dominic. "Could This Be the End of America's
Economic Supremacy?" *Daily Mail*, August 2, 2011.
Retrieved January 2012 (http://www.dailymail.co.uk
/debate/article-2021313/US-debt-crisis-Could-end
-Americas-economic-supremacy.html).

Shader, Maggie. "How a U.S. Debt Default Could Affect
You." ConsumerReports.org, July 29, 2011. Retrieved
February 2012 (http://news.consumerreports.org
/money/2011/07/how-a-us-debt-default-could-affect
-you.html).

Tepper, Hannah. "The Evolution of American Debt." Salon.
com, January 14, 2012. Retrieved February 2012
(http://www.salon.com/2012/01/14/the_evolution_of
_american_debt).

Waggoner, John. "What's Up with Europe's Economy—and Why You Should Care." *USA Today*, September 8, 2011. Retrieved January 2012 (http://www.usatoday.com/money/perfi/stocks/2011-09-08-europes-debt-crisis_n.htm).

Whitney, Meredith. "The Hidden State Financial Crisis." *Wall Street Journal*, May 18, 2011. Retrieved December 2011 (http://online.wsj.com/article/SB1000142405274870 34212045763291342618056612.html).

Index

About the Author

Philip Wolny is a writer and editor from Queens, New York. He has written on a variety of topics, including time spent as a financial trade journalist. He is the author of *Understanding Financial Frauds and Scams.*

Photo Credits

Cover (bank) © iStockphoto.com/Danil Melekhin; cover (headline) © iStockphoto.com/Lilli Day; cover (torn paper) © iStockphoto.com/Petek Arici; pp. 4–5, 8–9, 11, 23, 31, 33, 34, 36–37, 43, 45 © AP Images; pp. 7, 17, 30, 42, 54 © iStockphoto.com/Ivan Bliznetsov; pp. 13, 39, 60 Bloomberg/Getty Images; p. 15 Justin Sullivan/Getty Images; pp. 18–19 Getty Images; pp. 22, 24 Mark Wilson/Getty Images; pp. 26–27 Louisa Gouliamaki/AFP/Getty Images; p. 47 © Bruce R. Bennett/The Palm Beach Post/ZUMA Press; p. 50 © John Berry/Syracuse Newspapers/The Image Works; pp. 52–53 © Paul Rodriguez/The Orange County Register/ZUMA Press; pp. 56–57 Spencer Platt/Getty Images; pp. 62–63 Joshua Gunter/The Plain Dealer/Landov; p. 64 © iStockphoto.com/Peter Burnett.

Designer: Michael Moy; Editor: Kathy Kuhtz Campbell; Photo Researcher: Amy Feinberg